Addingham Houses
built in a time of village expansion
1750-1850

Arnold Pacey

Front cover: 40, Main Street

First published 2014
Second Edition published 2015 with the addition of the old photograph of North
Street (p.25), and related additions/adjustments to the text.

Published by
Addingham Civic Society
c/o The Old School,
Main Street, Addingham LS29 0NG
email: info@addinghamcivicsociety.co.uk

ISBN: 1502791269
ISBN-13: 9781502791269

PREFACE

The information about Addingham houses collected in this booklet arises from thirty years residence in the village during which observations of the buildings have slowly accumulated until they have begun to form a fairly coherent picture. Backing this up have been detailed surveys of some individual houses, a number of which were initiated by Kate Mason many years ago, and were carried out jointly by a group of us, including Kate herself, Alison Armstrong, Malcolm Birdsall and myself. Detailed reports on these surveys have been deposited in the archives of the Yorkshire Vernacular Buildings Study Group and the Yorkshire Archaeological Society, and several illustrations in this booklet have been extracted from these archive reports. Among these are the illustration of Fir Cottage on page vi, which is by Malcolm Birdsall, as is part of the illustration on p.16. Other line drawings are by the author, some made specially for this booklet, but others also from archive reports. I am very grateful indeed to all these colleagues and to occupants of houses who allowed us inside their homes.

The cover photographs are by Don Barrett. The photographs in the text are from the Addingham Digital Archive. The photo of the tomb of an important village craftsman in the churchyard (p.38) is by the author.

A.P.

Addingham

September 2014

CONTENTS

Page

Introduction   vii

PART ONE: THE OWNERS

1.1   Houses of the Cunliffe family   1

1.2   Cockshott houses & loomshops   7

1.3   The Spencers   13

1.4   Ebeneezer Jackson & John Brumfitt   15

1.5   Thomas Lister's barn & post office   19

1.6   The Wall family   23

PART TWO: THE BUILDERS

2.1   Introduction: The Builders of the houses   27

2.2   Richard Barritt   29

2.3   The Breare family   31

2.4   The Barkers   37

2.5   House near Townhead Mill   41

2.6   Lettering Styles   43

In Conclusion   47

FIR COTTAGE,
CHURCH STREET

Front elevation showing window and doorway dated 1677.
Evidence for an older house, possibly 14th century, has
been found in the roof and during alterations.

Drawing by Malcolm Birdsall, with his kind permission.

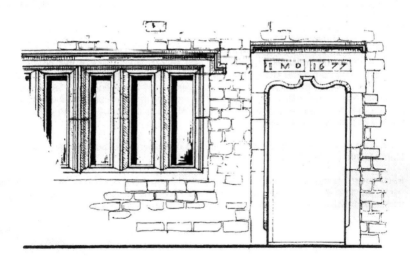

INTRODUCTION

The *oldest* houses in Addingham include some with medieval fragments of timber framing, such as Fir Cottage, Church Street (14th-century evidence), the Manor House, halfway up Main Street (c.1500), and a barn on Sugar Hill (where some fragments of timber from a late medieval house are visible from the road, reused as a lintel).

Then there is 17th-century stonework in some houses, as at Fir Cottage again (with doorway dated 1677, illustrated opposite), Low House, Sawmill Lane (which has plasterwork dated 1663 inside and 1675 on a datestone outside), and a doorway at the library (1669). A particularly striking house, and a nice example of its time, is 114 Main Street, accessed from Sugar Hill, where the doorway is dated 1730.

Except for this last house, the evidence for old construction on these sites is inconspicuous. The more prominent houses in the village tend to be later. Indeed, a high proportion of them, especially along Main Street, date from between 1750 and 1850, a time when the village was expanding rapidly as the textile industry developed.

Among Addingham houses of this period, some are notable for the role their owners played in village life, and some for the craftsmen responsible for their design and construction. The wealthiest owners during the 19th century were undoubtedly the Cunliffes and Cunliffe-Listers who made money from textile mills, including Low Mill and High Mill in Addingham, and Manningham Mill in Bradford, and invested much of it in land and houses in Addingham. Other, more modest, families whose houses we see in the Main Street include the Cockshotts, Spencers, Listers and Walls. When it comes to craftsmen and builders, the best documented is Joshua Breare, a stone-mason who was in charge of building the church tower in 1756-7 and who, with his son, built several of the 18th-century houses. Other notable masons were from the Spencer, Barker and Hargreaves families. These were all local builders, but a few houses were designed by masons or architects from outside the village, including the Old Rectory (by the mason Richard Barritt of Burley), and Hallcroft Hall (by a Leeds architect).

Part One: The Owners

1.1
HOUSES OF THE CUNLIFFE FAMILY

It makes sense to start with the owners of houses rather than the builders, and in particular with the Cunliffe family whose story in Addingham begins with a wool merchant named John Cunliffe and his wife Mary. John made enough money through trade and through partnerships in mills for his son William to live like a country gentleman at Farfield Hall, on the road to Bolton Abbey. The origins of the hall go back to around 1728 when the farmhouse formerly on the site was rebuilt in a very grand style by George Myers, former steward of the Earl of Burlington. The identity of the architect is unknown but Myers could himself have played a part in drawing up the design which includes giant fluted pilasters at the front and decoration derived from Chatsworth.[1]

---

1   Peter Leach and Nikolaus Pevsner, *The Buildings of England: Yorkshire, the West Riding, Leeds, Bradford and the North*, Yale University Press, 2009, p. 39. In Cliffe Castle Museum there is and extant notebooke that belonged to George Myers which seems to show him making calculations regarding sizes of windows.

CUNLIFFE COMMISSIONS from LEEDS ARCHITECTS

- the Church School, or Low School, 1844
  (now 7-9 North Street; a large name plaque above the entrance has
  been cut away)
- Hallcroft Hall, 1848

The Cunliffes owned Farfield Hall for about a century from about 1805, and in 1817 William Cunliffe was involved in landscaping the grounds to the south and the east by planting trees along the road and removing hedges to open up a number of small fields and clear the expanse of grass we see today in front of the hall.

Houses actually built for this family include High Bank House (46 Main Street) completed in 1790 for John and Mary Cunliffe (whose initials appear on the datestone). Further east, at the turning for High House Mews, there is 156 Main Street, which is the High House on whose grounds the mews houses were built. High House itself is, in part, older than it looks and there is a datestone inscribed 1752 at the back. The front was rebuilt when the house was remodelled about 1828 for Harriet Cunliffe (a daughter of John and Mary) at the time of her marriage to John Ellis, formerly of the City of London. The wide, but tall, mullioned windows with classical architraves are likely to have been designed by an architect from outside the village, not a local mason, but there is no information as to who this was.

Almost opposite is Beech Tree House, planned as three connected dwellings, 153-157 Main Street, and illustrated on the back cover. The design of the doorways, with shallow pilasters on either side and rather heavy lintels, looks as if it was simplified from the doorway design at High House, by the same architect. These houses were built for the Cunliffes in the 1820s, with one larger than the others having an open stair hall. This was the residence of Harriet Cunliffe's younger brother, Thomas Thompson Lister Cunliffe, a life-long bachelor.

At the east end of the village is another house built for the same brother about ten years earlier. Originally called Ashgate House, it is now known as Potters Hall, 63 Church Street. T.T.L.Cunliffe bought the land for it in 1815 and it was completed in 1817. It has an elegant interior with good panelled doors and window shutters. Facing Church Street, it has a good "Georgian" doorway (illustrated on the right on p. 40).

Another building project, though not a house, was construction of a church school on land given by the Cunliffes in 1844. Later, this became a National School, and was also known as the Low School, though eventually it was converted into houses, 7-9 North Street. Having apparently commissioned an architect rather than a local builder to design their alterations at High House, the Cunliffes - or the school committee they were supporting - again went to an architect, and the school was designed by the partnership of William Perkin and Elisha Backhouse of Leeds.[2]

The school comprises two linked ranges, one behind the other. A feature of the building now is the two chimneys that combine in a false gable above the entrance. An old photograph (illustrated p.25) shows that this structure was originally a tall bell turret.

Meanwhile, Harriet Cunliffe and her husband John Ellis, at High House, had been disturbed by a burglary, and by their proximity to the bustle of Main Street, and began to plan a new house. However, John died in 1847 before building began and, although Harriet was aged 67, she continued with the project on her own. She employed the same architects as had designed the school, Perkin and Backhouse, and the result was Hallcroft Hall. This has a symmetrical five-bay front with a central porch having "Roman Doric" columns that stand forward of the entrance, surmounted by lions probably made of artificial stone which was fashionable at the time. The roof has deep eaves and there are two chimney stacks towards the front, with two more at the back. Inside there is an open-well stair with cast-iron balusters (illustration, p.2).

Harriet had been in her forties when she married and did not have children. The 1851 census shows her living in the new house as a "landed proprietor" with three resident staff - cook, maidservant, and gardener/groom. One wonders at her building such a large house for such a small establishment, but she was able to enjoy it for a good many years before she died at the age of 86 in 1866. One problem, though, was smoke from the tall factory chimney at Low Mill, not far away across the fields, and she briefly refused to sign a lease for the tenant who was working the mill. But since the tenant's rent paid her bills, she soon changed her mind.[3]

One final building project to mention in connection with the Cunliffes and Cunliffe-Listers was at St Peter's Church where a burial vault for the family

2   Christopher Webster (ed.), *Building a great Victorian City: Leeds architects and architecture*, 2011, p. 390.
3   Kate Mason, *Woolcombers, Worsteds and Watermills*, Addingham Civic Society, 1989.

was constructed under a new vestry in 1857-8. This can be best appreciated today by walking round the east end of the church to the north side of the vestry where there is a plaque on the wall giving the names of those interred in the vault. Building the vestry and vault was linked to the rebuilding of the east wall of the church and a new east window was provided that is characteristic work by the architects employed, Mallinson and Healey of Bradford. Memorials to other members of the family can be seen inside the church, some on the walls, some in the form of stained glass by the artist William Holland of Warwick.

Stone for all the Cunliffe building projects, including High House, Hallcroft Hall and alterations at the church came from a quarry which has now merged into the landscape as a tree-lined gill at the bottom of the golf course but which was once variously known as Town Head Quarry or Vicar Wood Quarry. For many years it provided the best building stone used in the village and is mentioned again later as having belonged at one time to the Spencer family of masons and quarriers. It continued to be used into the twentieth century and provided stone for construction of the war memorial on Main Street.[4]

---

4   This information comes from the late Tom Mason, courtesy of Kate Mason.

88-94 Main Street, built for the Cockshotts in 1748. The building has been greatly altered, but the two doorways in the centre of the picture are characteristic of work by the mason Joshua Breare (p.9)

16-18 Church Street, probably built by Joshua Breare and his associates (p.17) *(photo: A. Pacey, c.1963)*

1.2
HOUSES & LOOMSHOPS BUILT FOR THE COCKSHOTT FAMILY

Having considered the few big residences in the village, we can turn to more typical village houses, beginning with the substantial number that were built to accommodate hand-loom weavers working for the Cockshott family. Three generations of this family commissioned new buildings, each favouring a slightly different style of architecture, so we can speak of early, middle and late phases in designs made for the Cockshotts.

John Cockshott (1706-1785) started life as a grocer but then began a series of enterprises in the cotton and wool industries, mostly to do with hand-loom weaving. His son, another John, developed the business further and also briefly entered into partnership with John Cunliffe to promote the construction of Low Mill. Cockshott had a house built at what is now 88 Main Street. It has since been greatly altered but the original doorway survives with a nicely carved lintel on which are John Cockshott's initials and those of his wife Martha with the date (illustration p.8). The carving is of high quality, and is so distinctive that we can say that it is the work of the mason Joshua Breare. It can be compared with a similar lintel made for another house owned by John and Martha at 82 Main Street, this time dated 1755.

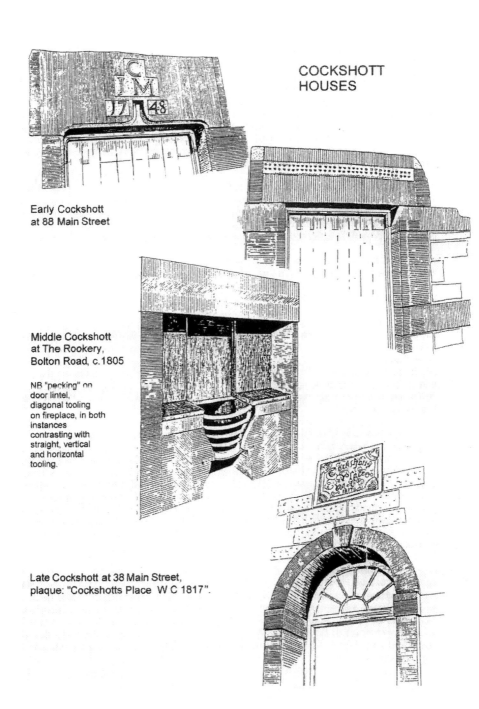

COCKSHOTT
HOUSES

Early Cockshott
at 88 Main Street

Middle Cockshott
at The Rookery,
Bolton Road, c.1805

NB "pecking" on
door lintel,
diagonal tooling
on fireplace, in both
instances
contrasting with
straight, vertical
and horizontal
tooling.

Late Cockshott at 38 Main Street,
plaque: "Cockshotts Place W C 1817".

In the generation following construction of these early Cockshott houses, John Cockshott's son, another John, developed the land behind them, first by adding more houses (one dated 1797), then by building a loomshop on Chapel Street.

The second John Cockshott also commissioned two blocks of formerly back-to-back cottages known as The Rookery on Bolton Road. These were built about 1805 and were intended to house hand-loom weavers, for whose use workshops were attached at the end facing Manor Garth (photograph on back cover). In contrast to the neat, regular finish of door lintels on the early Cockshott house at 88 Main Street (illustration p.6), the door lintels here have a patterned surface made partly with a broad chisel (broad tool), and partly with a point used to "peck" the surface, leaving small indentations.[5] Inside were some good stone fireplaces with similar tooling patterns (illustration opposite, based on the house in The Rookery known as 42 Bolton Road). This masonry finish and the heavy door lintels on which it appears are characteristic of what can be called a middle Cockshott style.

Meanwhile, a third generation of Cockshotts was emerging which included the original John Cockshott's grandsons and great-nephews. In their hands, the family textile business expanded further, still based on handlooms rather than factory work, and they built numbers of houses in Main Street for handloom weavers. The best of these were of quite distinguished design – the late Cockshott style – and include 30-38 Main Street (photo on page 46) with a datestone of 1817 on No.38 (Salt Pie Cottage). This carries the initials of William Cockshott and faces across a driveway to 40 Main Street (see front cover), another Cockshott house, which has the most elegant pedimented doorway in the village.

As the Cockshott business in hand-woven cloth expanded and as other enterprises grew, Martin and Samuel Cockshott saw the need for a warehouse to which weavers would deliver their finished pieces of cloth, and for a showroom or shop from which cloth could be sold. This was built about 1826 at 95-97 Main Street with the showroom facing the street.

---

5   The names of masons' tools and tooling patterns on stone are discussed and illustrated by Alison Armstrong in an article in the Yorkshire Vernacular Buildings Group Newsletter (*Yorkshire Buildings*), 18, 1990, pp.29-33.

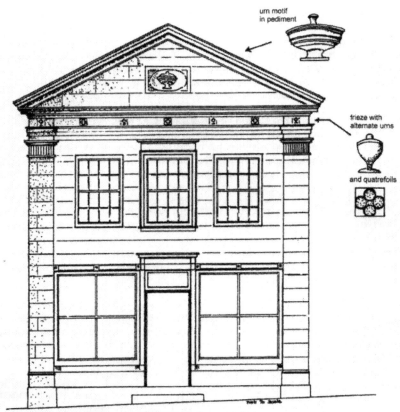

urn motif
in pediment

frieze with
alternate urns

and quatrefoils

97 Main Street: the Cockshotts' piece hall

LATE COCKSHOTT BUILDINGS

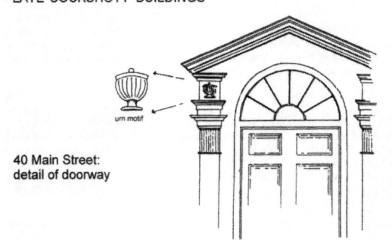

urn motif

40 Main Street:
detail of doorway

This building has just about the most imposing elevation in Main Street, with a pediment above tall pilasters at the corners, and large windows either side of the entrance. Within the pediment is a carved urn, and more urns and quatrefoils decorate the horizontal frieze above the first-floor windows (illustration opposite). It is the only building in Addingham to be illustrated in the Pevsner series of architecture reference books.[6]

The historian Kate Mason described this structure as the Cockshotts' "piece hall",[7] but production of cotton pieces on hand-looms was beginning a terminal decline and, soon after completion, the showroom was being used as a grocery store managed by a man named James Hudson. Later, and extending into the 1980s, it was a butcher's shop (photo p.36).

With regard to the architectural quality of the Cockshotts' buildings, there are interesting contrasts to be drawn between the early ones erected by the mason Joshua Breare with his associates (see chapter 2.3) and later buildings, culminating with the Piece Hall, and with the well-proportioned "Georgian" doorway at 40 Main Street which has a fanlight rising into its open pediment (illustrated opposite). The urn motif appears here again, and it seems likely that this is work by the same designer as the pediment at the Piece Hall. The houses behind the hall have doorways with the same kind of fanlights as in the Cockshotts' row of houses at 30-38 Main Street, and it could be that the same builders, probably the Barkers, were responsible for all these late Cockshott buildings.

6   Peter Leach and Nikolaus Pevsner, *The Buildings of England: Yorkshire West Riding, Leeds, Bradford and the North,* Yale University Press, 2009, plate 72.
7   Kate Mason, *Addingham from Brigantes to Bypass,* Addingham Civic Society, 1996, pp.87-9.

The Craven Heifer and 8 Main Street, 2010

1.3

THE SPENCERS OF THE CRAVEN HEIFER
AND DRUGGIST LANE

Most people in Addingham made their living from farming or, like the Cockshotts, from the textile industry. The Spencer family had members in almost every occupation apart from these – quarrying, building, inn-keeping, transport, pharmacy and coffee-roasting. In 1756, when the rebuilding of the church was being discussed, and construction of a tower was planned, Hugh Spencer agreed to supply the necessary stone from his quarry, which was in the gill at the bottom of what is now the golf course (see p.5). Hugh Spencer had four sons, one of whom, Thomas Spencer (1723-1780), worked as a mason and builder, while a nephew, George Spencer, leased the millstone quarry on Addingham Moorside.

William Spencer (1714-1803) was Hugh's oldest son and went into business as a carrier and inn-keeper at the Craven Heifer (opposite). Both activities entailed running a stable, and evidence of a smithy found at Spencer's house next to the Heifer is explained by the need to shoe horses regularly. The house, 8 Main Street, sometimes known as Craven Cottage, was built in

1762 and has the initials of William Spencer and his wife Susanna on the datestone. The Craven Heifer itself was rebuilt after 1800, but Craven Cottage remains as a nice example of masons' workmanship of the 1760s. The craftsman responsible was almost certainly William Spencer's brother Thomas, who went on to build The Crown at 136 Main Street in 1769. The Crown is recognisably the work of the same mason as Craven Cottage, and has a datestone in exactly the same style, and windows of somewhat taller proportions than were yet common in the village.

William and Susanna Spencer had three children, and they gave the name Marmaduke to the eldest, born in 1764. In later life he, like his father, became an innkeeper, and ran the King's Arms on Church Street (now a house, 25 Church Street). But he also began to develop a shop and general store on the corner of Main Street and what became Druggist Lane. In recent times, until 2014, this was a butcher's, but Marmaduke's son, William Spencer, had a business there selling medicines. Indeed, he was the druggist after whom Druggist Lane was named, and a building facing the lane was described as his "elaboratory" in a deed.

The whole block of buildings facing Main Street between Druggist Lane and Lodge Hill was erected for the Spencers as they developed their various businesses. One of the smaller houses, 133 Main Street, has a semicircular slab above the door on which was carved, before it weathered away, the date 1801 with initials of Marmaduke Spencer and his wife, with a lot of scroll-work decoration (illustrated p.44) . The building next door, on the corner of Lodge Hill, projects forward of the rest of the block, and was once a "coffee-roasting establishment" - the first coffee shop in Addingham - and later a sweet shop.[8]

---

[8] Initials on a fireplace inside this building are a modern copy of what appears on The Crown opposite, and do not date the house.

1.4
BUILDINGS FOR EBENEZER JACKSON
AND JOHN BRUMFITT

One owner of Farfield Hall in the years before the Cunliffes bought it was Ebenezer Jackson whose other properties, providing income from rents, included The Fleece Inn and the houses now known as 16-18 Church Street. He had all these rebuilt during the middle years of the 18th century, the work being done by Joshua Breare and his associates. Later, Breare built a reduced version of the Church Street houses on Brumfitt Hill, off Main Street (illustration overleaf).

At The Fleece, the entrance is at the centre of the elevation and opens into a lobby with a left turn into a bar and a right turn into a room with a large arched fireplace. The overall plan is square and symmetrical, with a dog-leg staircase in the centre at the back. Another room, plus stable, was built in a second phase of work, and the barn in a third phase. The Fleece was probably the oldest inn in Addingham, but after alterations were complete, its status was enhanced and it became a stopping place for the Leeds to Kendal stage coach.

THREE BUILDINGS OF c.1745-1755

House fronts, excluding attached barns, etc., are symmetrical about axis A-A'

The Fleece, Main Street, 1740s plus later additions

16-18, Church Street, c.1750

Scale of metres for
all three elevations

0 1 2 3 4 5   10

Brumfitt Hill, off Main Street, 1755

It is of considerable interest that Joshua Breare adapted the plans he had made for The Fleece when rebuilding the cottages Ebenezer Jackson owned in Church Street, c.1750. Little more was necessary to make the change than to provide two doorways at the front, and two dog-leg staircases at the back. The result was a pair of semi-detached houses, with the plan of one a mirror image of the other. One detail from The Fleece that did not fit this adaptation well was the window above the front door which, at Church Street, is made to light a closet belonging to one house in the pair that has no equivalent in the other. As at The Fleece, there is a connected barn, apparently built a year or two before.

The Breare group of masons had another opportunity to adapt the same design when they built a much smaller house with paired doorways in 1755. This looks like another semi-detached pair, and for many years was divided into two dwellings, but there is only one dog-leg staircase at the back (other stairs have been inserted), and a detailed survey found other evidence that this was built as a single house.

This dwelling is to be found between the Swan pub and the Old School where there is a turning off Main Street accessible only by pedestrians, with steps going up Brumfitt Hill, and the house is at the top. The Swan had not yet been built when this was completed and it may have functioned as a pub, with one doorway a public entrance and the other for the household only. The Brumfitts were described as inn-keepers and carriers, and had a horse-drawn wagon that made regular trips to York, delivering parcels and small loads.[9]

The two front doorways of the Brumfitts' house have one lintel carved with the date, 1755, and the other with the initials of John Brumfitt and his wife. It is significant that neither The Fleece nor the Church Street house has a carved date or any ornamentation, presumably because Ebenezer Jackson was a Quaker. The Brumfitt door lintels have the same decorative detail as the "early Cockshott" lintel illustrated earlier, confirming that they are work by Joshua Breare. The windows have chamfered mullions set back slightly from the face of the wall and look very traditional, even old-fashioned, for 1755.

---

[9]   An accident with the York wagon led to the death of Ellis Brumfitt: Ilkley Parish Register, entry for 1792.

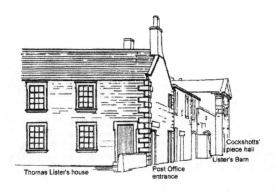

THOMAS LISTER'S
HOUSE & BARN
99-103 Main Street

left: Sketch showing
relationship of house to
barn and other buildings

below:
Elevation of barn

bottom:
Masons' tooling
patterns on barn

Cockshotts'
piece hall

Lister's Barn

Post Office
entrance

Thomas Lister's house

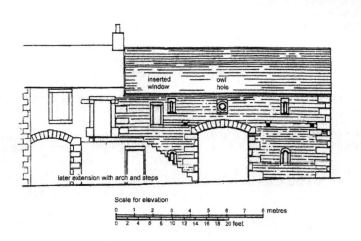

inserted
window

owl
hole

later extension with arch and steps

Scale for elevation

0 1 2 3 4 5 6 7 8 metres
0 2 4 6 8 10 12 14 16 18 20 feet

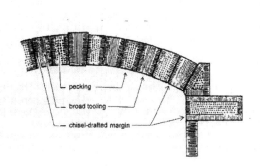

pecking

broad tooling

chisel-drafted margin

broad
tooling
on face
of lintel

chamfer

1.5
THOMAS LISTER'S BARN & POST OFFICE

Opposite Brumfitt Hill, on the other side of Main Street, was a property owned by Thomas Lister which, a little later, became the post office. This was run for years by descendants of Lister, so it has to be explained that there were several families with this surname in Addingham, and the Listers at the post office were not related to the Cunliffe Listers.

The first Thomas Lister was described as a tallow-chandler, which meant that he was a dealer in candles, raw tallow and, probably, soap. It is known, for example, that the candles used in St Peter's Church were usually bought from him.[10] Like most small traders in Addingham, he also kept a few cows, which grazed on land he owned behind the Sailor pub. When he built a barn, now converted to a house at 99 Main Street, it included a mistal (shippon) in which the cows could be milked. However, as Main Street became more built-up, keeping cows there became more difficult and the main function of the barn became to keep the horses Lister needed to go about his business, to store their fodder, and to be a warehouse for candles and tallow.

---

[10] Addingham Churchwardens' Accounts, Bradford Archives, BDP 1/7/1/2, e.g. 1808, 1s 1d paid for candles.

Thomas Lister built his barn in 1777, one year after his brother, William Lister, had built a similar barn at Small Banks, on Addingham Moorside. Both barns were to the same design, except that the one at Small Banks was somewhat longer. It is also clear that the same stone masons built both because the decorative tooling with which lintels and quoins were finished is rather elaborate, and closely similar on both buildings. In each case, the doorway to the stable carries the date. This reads L/TM 1777 on Lister's barn in Main Street, the third initial being that of Thomas's wife Martha (formerly Martha Cockshott).

Each barn has a wide cart entrance under an archway with a prominent keystone, and with alternative stones in the arch-ring decorated with either broad tooling or pecking. Comparison with other work by Joshua Breare's son, who had the same name and is referred to here as Joshua II, suggests that he built these barns.

This same tooled decoration may provide a clue to the origins of tooling previously noted at The Rookery, Bolton Road, and characterised as a "middle Cockshott" phase in local building traditions. It is probable that Joshua II, with others, was responsible for this decoration also. The fact that this particular tooling pattern was used quite prolifically in Addingham for twenty years and then ceased about 1805, the year Joshua II died, may confirm that it was a personal preference of his.

Thomas Lister lived at 103 Main Street, a house that was rebuilt about 1799, the year his son, another Thomas, was married to Mary Wall. The house has its gable end on the street and faces a small garden occupying the space between the building and Town Beck. The front of the house is distinguished by its classical design, the windows and doorways having moulded architraves, and one wonders if it was built by masons from outside the village. If it was built by masons of the Breare family, they were unusually restrained with regard to tooling patterns.

There are two doorways in the symmetrical house front, one at either end. The doorway nearest the street became an entrance to the post office, because Thomas Lister the younger, while continuing the tallow and candle business, became postmaster for Addingham just before 1800. Quite soon, though, new doorways were made in the gable end so that the post office could be entered direct from the street without customers coming through the garden.

Another enterprise in which the two Thomas Listers, father and son, became involved was prospecting for coal, because they had the idea that there was coal in the hillside where they grazed their cows. A little coal had been found higher up the hill at Gildersber, and they made contact with a Mr. Cox who claimed to have found a 2-ft seam in the area. In the 1840s, a pit was sunk on the Listers' land south of The Sailor, but without any result.[11]

During the time Thomas Lister was postmaster, mail from London came up the Great North Road to Wetherby where horses were changed before the coach continued north. From Wetherby, another coach travelled overnight via Otley to Addingham and then on to Skipton, leaving letters for Addingham and Bolton Abbey at Lister's post office about 8 a.m.[12] Letters going in the other direction were collected from the post office at 3 p.m., presumably by the same coach returning to Wetherby. This system continued until the first railways were built, when the mail was taken to the nearest station, initially Steeton.[13]

The Lister family ran Addingham post office for 130 years in all, with Thomas Lister succeeded as postmaster by his son, William, and then by his grand-daughter, Sarah.[14] When the compulsory registration of births and deaths was introduced in 1837, William Lister also served as registrar for the village, succeeded by "Miss S.M. Lister", until the latter retired as postmistress in 1928 after 46 years service. It was then that the post office moved to the location sandwiched between George Street and Main Street where it remained until 2015. More recently, the Listers' house was familiar to many people through its use as the doctor's surgery, for around forty years until the present health centre opened.

---

[11] I am indebted to Will Varley for this information. See also Kate Mason, *Addingham from Brigantes to Bypass*, Addingham Civic Society, 1996, p. 92.

[12] There was much mail for Bolton Abbey when the Duke of Devonshire was in residence.

[13] Ronald Ward, *The Postal History of Upper Wharfedale, Ilkley and Otley*, Yorkshire Postal History Society, 1972, pp.54-6. The railway did not reach Ilkley until 20 years after it got to Steeton.

[14] There is some uncertainty about this name; it could have been Susan rather than Sarah.

DATESTONES
at one time to be
seen in North Street

Henry Wall 1852
badly weathered
at No. 8.

George & Margaret
Brayshaw 1793
from house now
demolished on
site of the garden
at No. 15.

Scale for both drawings

1.6
THE WALL FAMILY OF HIGH MILL & THEIR HOUSES IN MAIN STREET

High Mill was the village corn mill from as early as the 14th century when its long weir crossing the River Wharfe at an oblique angle was first built. In the 1780s, the small, early mill was greatly extended with the new part used as a water-powered spinning mill while the older part continued to function as a corn mill.

The extension of the mill is well documented and is described in Kate Mason's books, but information is lacking for a time in the 1790s and around 1800, and the story only becomes clearer after the Wall family were established as millers and, in 1812, when they rebuilt the mill house. This house stands on Bolton Road at the junction with High Mill Lane and is of restrained design with loosely classical proportions but with little ornamentation apart from the datestone, which is marked with the initials HWM. The middle initial is raised to show that it represents the surname, Wall, while the others stand for Henry and Mary.

After this there is another gap in the record until 1817 when Thomas and John Wall had taken over and were the millers. At this time, the corn mill was producing oatmeal from locally-grown oats, and flour from wheat that they brought in from farms in the Vale of York or perhaps further away. The Walls also dealt in barley that was used for making malt and hence for brewing beer, and they managed the malt kiln hidden away behind 140

Main Street, the shop now known as The Olive Branch. For a time another member of the Wall family, Richard, was landlord of The Fleece at a time when pubs often brewed their own beer and therefore used the malt produced almost next door. Richard Wall died in 1833 and was succeeded at The Fleece by William Wall. Unfortunately, there is no family tree to show how these different members of the family were related, but it is striking how their business interests in grain, flour, malt and beer interlocked.

The Wall family also built houses near to their businesses, including 144 Main Street, with the initials of William and Dorothy Wall on the datestone of 1812, and opposite, a pair of three-storey, semi-detached houses, 143-145 Main Street. These are dated 1826 and have a very different appearance owing to their tall proportions, prominent quoins, and doorways with semicircular fanlights.

Another member of the Wall family in the next generation was Henry Wall, a butcher. He bought houses in North Street as an investment. They were small - one room on each of two floors - but he enlarged two of them, 8 and 10 North Street (datestone illustrated p.22), by building outwards and taking a width of five feet from what had been tiny front gardens and the margins of the road. That made it possible to provide a separate kitchen equipped with a wash-copper (or set-pot) behind the main living room and a second bedroom upstairs. At the top of the hill, at the edge of the steep drop down to the river, were shared earth closets and an "ash place" where ash from the coal fires was dumped, some of it being sprinkled into the earth closets to keep down flies and smells.

At one time there were cottages on both sides of North Street, as can be seen from the photograph opposite, which also shows the school on the left. The earliest is thought to have been built about 1760, and one certainly had a datestone inscribed 1767. Others were built at irregular intervals forming a long row on the east side of the narrow road and a smaller number on the west side.

A few of the cottages were built by the Overseers of the Poor to accommodate destitute people, but most were built by private landlords, including the only two that still stand (8-10 North Street). The Overseers contracted with a mason named James Pickard to build two further cottages in 1825, although it is not clear which these were. All these dwellings were of rubble stone, but Henry Wall's extension to numbers 8-10 had internal walls of locally-made brick and the front wall was of good watershot masonry. Inside, fittings included doors made of tongue-and-groove boards and simple panelled partitions round the head of the stairs, all nice examples of country carpentry. It is significant that these two houses were the only ones spared when the rest of the row was demolished for "slum clearance" in the 1960s.

There was a datestone above the door of 8 North Street inscribed with Henry Wall's initials and the date 1852. The numbers on the datestone have now weathered to the point where they are illegible except in favourable light, but before the weathering got too bad, they were examined closely from a ladder and a tracing was made. Later, a small modern extension to the house was provided with a new datestone repeating the figures from the old one along with the date of the extension: "1852+1995".

The very simple style of sans-serif lettering used on this house makes an interesting comparison with a datestone made sixty years earlier for a house that once stood almost opposite, on a site that is now the garden of 15 North Street (both datestones illustrated p.22).

Old postcard showing North Street in about 1900 (school on extreme left)

ADDINGHAM BUILDERS AND MASONS, 1750-1851

Masons named in building accounts, contracts, vestry minutes, etc.	Masons named in Addingham parish registers	Masons named in Baines's directory, 1822 (and Pigot's directory, 1834)	Masons, builders, brick-makers/layers, in the census, 1851
Joshua Breare (I)[1, 2] Joshua Breare (II)[4] William Hustwick[2]	Joshua Breare (I, 1707-63) Joshua Breare (II, 1746-1805) *Joshua Breare (III, 1781-1815)[8] *James Breare (b. 1793) *Francis Breare (b.1797) *Samuel Breare (1798-c.1845) Joshua Breare (IV, b. 1811)[8] Joshua Breare (V, b. 1823)[8] [*sons of Breare II]	James Breare (1822) Francis Breare (1834) Samuel Breare (1822)	Isabella Breare,[7] aged 49, widow, brick & tile maker, employer of 7 men. Joshua Breare (IV),[8] mason Joshua Breare (V),[8] master stone mason
Thomas Spencer[2]	Thomas Spencer (1713-1780)		
John Hargreaves I[2] John Hargreaves II[3] William Hargreave[5]	John Hargreaves (I, 1730-1808) John Hargreaves (II, 1761-1794) William Hargreaves (b. 1765)		
James Bradley[4]	James Bradley, of Small Banks, fl.1788-1800, related to the Breares by marriage		
William Bland[4]	William Bland, Small Banks		
	Thomas Beck (I, 1713-1797) Thomas Beck (II, b.1745) John Beck (b. 1809)	no Becks in directories	John Beck, master builder employing 20 men & 3 apprentices.
Richard Barritt[5] William Barritt[5]	no masons of this name in Addingham; Barritt was from Burley		
James Pickard[6]	James Pickard (b. 1790)		
	Peter Barker (I, 1749-1805) James Barker (1773-1814) Joseph Barker (1783-1828) Peter Barker (II, 1792-1833) John Barker (b. 1802)	Joseph Barker (1822) Peter Barker (1822)	John Barker, age 49, journeyman stone mason
	moved to Addingham c.1825?	William Gale (1834)	William Gale, born in Ireland, journeyman mason
	William Lister (b. 1813), son of James Lister, carpenter	no Listers in directories	William Lister, stone mason, employing 4 men

Notes: 1. Agreement to build a barn at Hag Head, Chelker, 1742 (quoted by Marie Hartley)
2. Contract, accounts for building St Peter's church tower, rebuilding south wall, 1756-7
3. Building Low Mill, 1787 (see Kate Mason, Woolcombers, etc.,)
4. Extending High Mill, 1788 (see Smith of Addingham papers, YAS, DD 61)
5. Faculty, contract and accounts for building new rectory, 1806-8 (Borthwick Institute, York)
6. Building two cottages for destitute people, 1825, Addingham Overseers of the Poor.
7. Isabella Breare, born Isabella Parker, was the widow of Samuel Breare.
8. Joshua III was a son of Joshua II; Joshua IV was his grandson, and Joshua V was his nephew

Part Two: The Builders

2.1
BUILDERS OF THE HOUSES: ADDINGHAM
STONE MASONS

In 1822, Edward Baines's trade directory, listing businesses in this part of
the West Riding, included the names of five stone masons based in
Addingham. Three were members of the Breare family, and the other two
were Joseph and Peter Barker. No architects were listed, the majority of
houses being designed by the masons who built them in discussion with the
owners.

Masons listed in this way were often running small building firms or
companies, though so informally organised that they are now hard to
identify. Many other masons can be identified from the parish register
where their names and occupations were recorded when they married or
died, or when their children were baptised (see table opposite). Some, such
as James Pickard, were working on too small a scale to be in Baines's
directory, and others are identified in census returns as journeymen masons
which usually means that they were employees of somebody else, and there
were also apprentices. Sons often took up the same trade as their fathers,
so there were several families of masons such as the Breares, the Barkers,
the Becks and the Hargreaves.

Although the directory shows that the Barker and Breare families were the leading builders in Addingham in 1822, Pigot's directory of 1834 mentions nobody from the Barker family, and by the time of the 1851 census there was only one journeyman mason with this family name. By then much the largest firm was that of Thomas Beck, who was described as employing 20 men and 3 apprentices. But although we can name masons and builders in this way there are very few documents to say who built which house.

OLD RECTORY,
Low Mill Lane

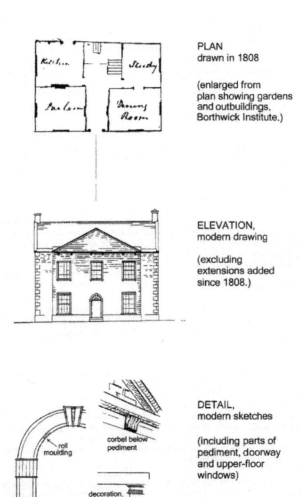

PLAN
drawn in 1808

(enlarged from
plan showing gardens
and outbuildings,
Borthwick Institute.)

ELEVATION,
modern drawing

(excluding
extensions added
since 1808.)

DETAIL,
modern sketches

(including parts of
pediment, doorway
and upper-floor
windows)

roll
moulding

corbel below
pediment

decoration,
upper floor
windows

2.2
RICHARD BARRITT AND THE RECTORY

The only well documented house of the period is the Old Rectory, in extensive grounds on Low Mill Lane to the east of the church. Its construction in 1806-8 is recorded among church "faculties" held by the Borthwick Institute of Historical Research, University of York, which include a rough plan (illustrated opposite). The document shows that the builder was not a mason from the village but was Richard Barritt from Burley-in-Wharfedale.

Before extensions were added on the west and east sides, the house had a symmetrical south front with a pediment on carved corbels. The front door, at the centre of the elevation, has a fanlight like several houses in the village and the contract with the builder shows that this was the result of a choice between a doorway design at Farfield Hall, and a doorway at "Jas Bond's house". It was the second example that was taken as the model, but the detailing is quite unlike any other building in the village.

Among outbuildings at the back, at a time when better-off householders would produce their own beer, was a brewhouse, built later under a different contract by a mason named John Hargreaves. He was the son of a man named Hargreaves who had worked on the church in the 1750s, the Hargreaves being another local family of masons.

Extracts from two pattern books
by Batty Langley

1)
*The City and Country Builder's Treasury
of Designs*, 1745

Font, rather like a garden bird-bath, likely to be
the inspiration for the font in St Peter's Church.

Doorway, a design perhaps used in designing
High Bank House, 46 Main Street,
for John and Mary Cunliffe, 1790

2)
The Builder's Director, or Bench-mate, 1751

Designs for the keystone of an arch, used
for doorways at St Peter's Church, c.1756-7
and for the arched doorway of a barn
at Small Banks, Addingham Moorside, 1776

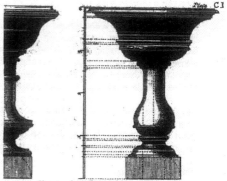

Fonts for Churches

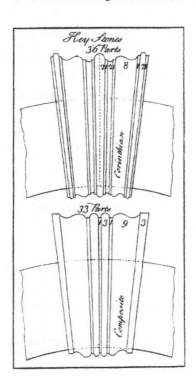

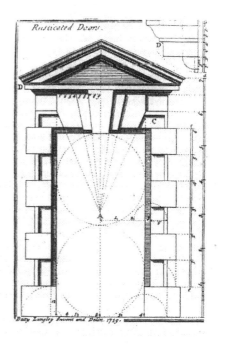

2.3
THE BREARE FAMILY

There are a mere handful of documents which identify masons who worked on the construction of mills and barns (rather than houses), of which the earliest describes the building of a barn in 1742 at Hag Head, near Chelker, off the road to Skipton. This barn no longer exists, but is described clearly in the document which shows that the builder was the mason Joshua Breare (c.1707-1763).[15] Apart from this and the Old Rectory, the only project for which there are detailed building accounts or contracts is work done at St Peter's Church in 1756-57 when the south wall was rebuilt and the tower constructed.

Four masons who worked on the church are mentioned, including Joshua Breare who made drawings and was generally in charge. But although the agreement mentions the four men individually they seem to have done so much work together that they were like an informally organised building firm. For example, one of the other masons, apart from Breare, was William Hustwick from Draughton, who appears in accounts for buildings higher up the valley where he was also working with Joshua Breare.[16] These two masons are mentioned together sufficiently often to suggest that they were business partners, though they are never referred to as such. The other masons working on the church, John Hargreaves and Thomas Spencer, may have been other informal partners. There is evidence to

---

[15] This document is quoted by Marie Hartley and Joan Ingilby, *Dales Memories*, 1986.
[16] I am indebted to Brontë Bedford Payne and Heather Beaumont for information about Joshua Breare's work in Barden.

suggest friendship between Spencer and Breare, and they could well have worked together throughout the 1750s. Spencer took on a job independently when his brother asked him to build Craven Cottage in 1762, as mentioned on page 13 above. He then built The Crown after Breare died.

The large number of well-built houses dating from 1748-1760 that have Breare characteristics are hard to credit to just one leading mason, and it becomes easier to understand how so much was achieved if these men were regularly worked as a group. Their workforce would include many others who appear in parish records as "labourers" and are hard to distinguish from farm labourers.

After Joshua Breare died in 1763, his rather conservative style of house design, with mullioned windows and his trade-mark door lintels, was immediately dropped. Meanwhile, John Hargreaves and other masons in his family specialised in more utilitarian kinds of structure including mills and the brewhouse at the Old Rectory. One hypothesis is that William Hargreaves did building for the Wall family at High Mill and at the malt kiln.

Joshua Breare's son, Joshua Breare II (1746-1805), was still a teenager when his father died but several houses and barns built later in the 18th century can be attributed to him partly because he seems to have continued using his father's drawings and pattern books, as at the Wesleyan Methodist meeting house on Chapel Street (now flats) where, in 1778, he made two doorways that repeat the design of the south doorway at St Peter's Church (with simplifications), but keeping to exactly the same dimensions.

In his work at the church, it is evident that the senior Breare was using one of several pattern books by Batty Langley. The font at St Peter's is derived from one illustrated by Langley and other details from the book are repeated in one or two Addingham buildings likely to have been built or altered by Joshua Breare II (see illustration p.30). But what also seems characteristic of the latter, and of masons working with him, was elaborate tooling patterns such as those on door lintels at The Rookery (illustrated p. 8).

At the end of the century, Breare II was something of a public figure in the village and was a churchwarden. But numerous buildings that show signs of his involvement were also going up, so he must have had several men working with him, perhaps including members of the Beck and Barker families of masons. Some of the best work in his style is at Small Banks on Addingham Moorside, and a mason living and probably working there was James Bradley, whose wife was related to the Breares.

What is noticeable about the Breare group's architecture is that, although they worked in a classical manner at St Peter's Church in 1756-7, and used pattern books that illustrated classical detail, their houses retained many traditional or vernacular features, including the tooling patterns mentioned. After Joshua II died in 1805, it is noticeable that this style of tooling was less used and there was no longer an obvious Breare style in the village.

However, moving forward forty years, one small house did have some very individual work by one of the later Breares, though it disappeared during alterations in 2001. The house stands at the junction of Chapel Street, Back Beck Lane, and Long Riddings Lane, and is known as 10 Chapel Street. It is the house where Samuel Breare and his wife Isabella lived. They are the family members who established a brick-making business and, although Samuel died in the 1840s, the house was still occupied by Isabella at time of the 1851 census when she was running the business. The census recorded her as: "Isabella Breare, brick and tile manufacturer, employing 7 men".

This house, now altered beyond recognition, had an L-shaped plan with a rear wing that may have been used as a woolcomber's or blacksmith's workshop early in the 19th century. The main front, facing south, was gabled with the main doorway in the centre of the elevation. It had been extended, possibly by Samuel, to form an enormously wide and high gable topped with a stack and five red chimney pots (perhaps made in the tile kiln). Above the doorway was a sundial with the date, 1841, an inscription, and two sets of initials: SB for Samuel Breare and GP, probably for a George Prior, a clockmaker who had expertise in the design of sundials. Wording at the top of the sundial may be a quotation: "Al[l times have their e]nd / pr[ogress has its] term",[17] but much of the lettering had weathered away long before the sundial was removed and the building was extended.

---

[17] A small prize is offered for a more plausible interpretation and source of the quotation.

Samuel Breare's house, 10 Chapel Street

South elevation and, below, sun-dial formerly over the door.
(Drawing made about 2.30 in the afternoon, as shown by
the shadow.)

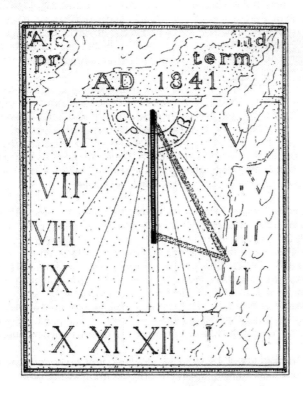

Much more could be said about the Breares, including those who dropped the final e from their name, built up a chair making business, and ran the saw-mill down to the year 2000, and others who retained the e and continue to work in building design, notably in Silsden.

The Piece Hall as Terry Smith's butchers in 1966

2.4

THE BARKERS AND THE PIECE HALL DESIGNER

Samuel Breare's house (illustrated p.34) was an oddity on a back lane. As to more prominent houses on Main Street, few can be attributed to the Breares because, after the death of the second Joshua Breare in 1805, his several sons were too young to take charge of his business. Samuel, at that time, was aged only 7. So a new trend in house design emerged as other masons took the lead, and as the Cockshott family in particular commissioned houses for their workers from masons with a different outlook.

Houses that reflect this trend have taller proportions, and their rooms have higher ceilings displaying different ideas about interior design. Sometimes, for example, there are arched alcoves for shelves, or there are built-in cupboards with moulded timber architraves. Other woodwork commonly seen includes window shutters folding back into panelled window reveals, and good panelled doors. There were several joiners in the village capable of such work, including members of the Guyer family, and employees of John England, a carpenter who was a prominent member of the village community and is commemorated by an elaborately lettered box tomb in the churchyard (photo p.38).

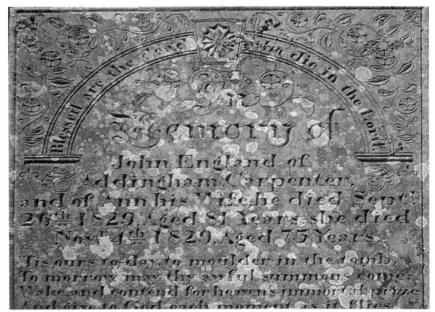

John England's tomb

The most distinctive feature of these houses, nearly all dating from c.1805-1830, is that there is often a semicircular fanlight above the front door such as the one already noted at the Old Rectory, though without the mouldings used there.

More typical houses with fanlights for which a date can be quoted are numbers 38 and 143-5 Main Street (respectively 1817 and 1826). In another three especially notable houses, there is not only a fanlight above the door but it is sheltered by an open pediment and pilasters on either side, creating what is often regarded as a typical Georgian doorway. One of these houses, 63 Church Street (Potters Hall), can be dated by a deed and a map that show it was built between 1815 and 1817. Another, at 9 Main Street, may be a year or two later.

Both these are notably elegant houses in their proportions and internal fittings but their pedimented doorways are not quite "correct" in their proportions. They have a slightly squashed appearance with the fanlights reduced from semicircular to segmental or semi-elliptical shapes (illustrated p.40). They give the impression of having been made by craftsmen who were not entirely at home with classical architecture. However, a third pedimented doorway at 40 Main Street (illustrated p.10 & front cover) suggests the work of a builder who had gained more experience and greater confidence. It has engaged columns either side of the doorway with more substantial capitals and an entablature decorated with a tiny urn-shape. There is a higher pediment that allows for a more regularly shaped fanlight.

This doorway is so well-designed and executed as to raise the suspicion that it is the work of somebody who had worked on a relatively sophisticated building elsewhere. If he was a local man, he was perhaps somebody who had served an apprenticeship with an experienced master mason, or who had travelled and seen quality work in other places.

Baines's Directory of 1822 mentioned five leading masons in Addingham of whom two were from the Barker family and three were Breares, and it is possible that the mason (or masons) who made these doorways were one or other of them. A clue is that many of the houses with fanlights were built for the Cockshott family. The Cockshotts had business interests outside Addingham, notably at Baildon, so it is possible that they had employed an Addingham mason on a project there that gave him wider experience than he would get if he always worked in his home village.

Parish register entries for 1818 show that Joseph Barker, normally resident in Addingham, was working in Baildon that year, and it could be that he was doing work there for the Cockshotts. This and other circumstantial evidence leads to the view that Joseph Barker and other masons in his family, perhaps with such colleagues as Thomas Beck II, may have been responsible for most of the later Cockshott buildings, including 40 Main Street.

Whoever the craftsmen were, their work can be recognised again in the Cockshott "Piece Hall", 97 Main Street (photo on p.36), built about 1826, where the imposing pediment has an urn shape in its decoration and repeats several other details that are also seen at 40 Main Street.

9 MAIN STREET

FRONT DOORWAY
(north elevation, c.1815-20)

semi-elliptical
fanlight within
open pediment

simplified capital
(compared with
over-large detail
at Church Street)

flat pilaster
(compared with
rounded
half-column
at Church Street)

plinth of minimal
height

63 CHURCH STREET
(doorway of 1815-17)

BACK DOORWAY
(south elevation, earlier than
front, c.1750)

rounded
corner
(Breare
style)

joint in stonework at
what was the end of
the house in c.1750

DOOR LINTEL IN OUTBUILDING
at 9 Main Street

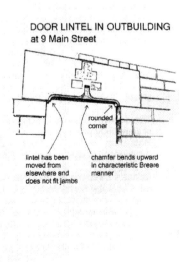

lintel has been
moved from
elsewhere and
does not fit jambs

chamfer bends upward
in characteristic Breare
manner

rounded
corner

2.5
A HOUSE NEAR TOWNHEAD MILL

The assertively classical architectural style of the Piece Hall and the houses with pedimented doorways is in marked contrast to what was built by the earlier Breare group of masons. The Breares could work in a classical style when required, using pattern books to guide them, but reverted to a more vernacular approach when left to themselves – as exemplified by Joshua Breare I's continued use of mullioned windows and Joshua II's tooling patterns.

One house that demonstrates the contrast in architectural style between early 19th century houses with their fanlights and the earlier work attributed to Joshua Breare I and his associates is the former mill-owner's house near Town Head Mill at 9 Main Street. The back wall of the house, which faces south, has many alterations where windows have been enlarged, but the doorway is older, and is set in old masonry showing a joint in the stonework where the building was extended (bottom left in the illustration opposite), and the door jambs and lintel have the narrow chamfer and rounded corner detail that one sees in many Breare buildings.

At right angles to the house at its west end is a former stable and other outbuildings, and a doorway on their west side has a lintel of the kind that is characteristic of Joshua Breare, with a narrow chamfer that turns upward like an ogee at the centre of the lintel (bottom right p.40). It does not fit the jambs that support it and looks as if it was moved from a different location. Further study of these buildings, including a surviving mullioned window, shows that the complex could well have developed from a house built in the 1750s. As it is, the front of the house, facing Main Street, has a pedimented doorway with a fanlight and windows with Georgian proportions, and inside, the woodwork is of the quality seen in other houses with these features, except where it has been altered in the late 20th century.

So it seems that there may have been a house here that was built by Joshua Breare in the middle years of the 18th century. Then its front wall was rebuilt some time around 1815-20 in the manner that can probably be associated with the Barker family of masons. When it came to replacing Breare's doorway by the one with the fanlight, instead of breaking up the lintel, the builders moved it to the outbuilding and chiselled off the initials of a previous owner along with the date. But some faint curves remain suggesting that the date was one whose last two digits were rounded at the bottom, so the date may have been 1760.

2.6
LETTERING STYLES

As well as noticing the distinctive architecture that appeared in Addingham during this period, it is worth studying the carved lettering and decoration used on stonework as another aspect of design. The contrast between sans-serif and Roman lettering that could once be seen on datestones in North Street has already been mentioned. The datestone of 1793 from North Street, illustrated on page 22, is very much the kind of lettering used earlier by the Breares, as seen on the door lintel of 1748 illustrated on page 8. Another example, with the date 1785, is from a farmhouse at Small Banks on Addingham Moorside, and is illustrated on page 44.

A feature of this datestone and the similar one from North Street is the circular wheel pattern on either side of the top initial. This could be inspired by another illustration in a Batty Langley pattern book, which includes a flower carved in stone with petals whirled around in a manner that has been reduced to simple curves in these carvings.

Another kind of lettering altogether is at 38 Main Street, where a stone above the door has the initials of William Cockshott and the date 1817 inscribed using idiosyncratic lettering with elaborate flourishes, while in the

SMALL BANKS,
Addingham
Moorside

plaque framed in
stone on a farmhouse
with initials of Richard
and Sarah Shackleton

38 MAIN STREET

plaque (in perspective)
with initials of William
Cockshott, date 1817,
and: "Cockshotts Place"

DATES ON HOUSES
CUT IN STONE

133 MAIN STREET

panel over door with
initials of Marmaduke
and Mary Spencer
(lettering now flaked
and weathered away)

corners of this rectangular plaque are decorative fan shapes that are reminiscent of the Adam style (opposite). Similar details occur on gravestones in the churchyard of around the same date, including some elaborate box tombs and table tombs.

There are also two much simpler gravestones commemorating members of the Barker family of masons, including one discussed on page 48. Much of the lettering on this stone is in a plain Roman style, but at the top are idiosyncratic letters and flourishes as on the house datestone just mentioned. This presumably reflects the taste of the Barkers.

Thus although there are no building contracts that demonstrate which houses were built by this family of masons, there are clues here as to which datestones they may have cut. A dated stone panel at 133 Main Street is now too badly weathered to be legible, but a record made before it got so bad (illustrated opposite) shows Marmaduke Spencer's initials with elaborate curves and tendrils playing on the initial S. The plain Roman initials M are for Marmaduke and his wife, Mary. Mention can also be made of the elaborate flourishes, scrolls and an arch shape on the gravestone of John England, the leading carpenter in the village (see photograph p.38).

Hence, as well as the different architectural styles associated with the Breare group of masons and the Barkers, there were different tastes in lettering. Many other masons and house-owners were content with plain and simple Roman lettering, as on the datestone at The Crown (overleaf), probably by Thomas Spencer, or on the Wall family house at 144 Main Street.

30-38 Main Street

The Crown in 1996

IN CONCLUSION

This survey of houses built in Addingham between 1750 and 1850 has identified two particularly distinctive groups of buildings – those associated with Joshua Breare I that were built between 1748 and his death in 1763 – and those probably connected with the Barker masons and constructed between the turn of the century and, it seems, the deaths of Joseph Barker in1828 and Peter Barker II in 1833.

In between the first Breare and the Barkers, a somewhat less well defined group of houses includes some that seem certain to have been built by Breare's son, Joshua II, and several others likely to have been built by his employees or associates, including James Bradley. Two houses of the 1760s, one of them The Crown, can also be attributed to the mason Thomas Spencer.

After that, and particularly after the years when the Barkers were busy, there are fewer houses with such strongly distinctive characteristics that they can be attributed to individual masons. However, the rise of the Beck family, who comprised the largest building firm in Addingham in 1851, must account for several. The history of this family is that, in the 1750s, Thomas Beck I was a neighbour of Joshua Breare I, and is likely to have worked for him, and then with Joshua II, notably in extending the Methodist meeting house on Chapel Street, at which Beck was a member. Later, there are hints that Beck's son may have built houses for the Wall family, perhaps beginning with 144 Main Street in 1812. After that, it is likely that quite a number of the well-built houses that lack datestones were built by the Becks.

This is a rather general picture because of the lack of paper documents such as contracts or building accounts (except at the Old Rectory). But another kind of document, not made of paper, comprises the stone plaques and dated door lintels on which were carved the initials of house-owners. Datestones can be misleading where they have been moved, but most of those in Addingham belong to the houses where they can still be seen and do reliably show the date of at least part of the structure to which they are attached. The initials on them can also, nearly always, be correlated with names in the parish register and on the schedule to the parish rating map of 1817. These two documents provide a key to the carved initials and much additional data as well.

Since so much information is conveyed by datestones, and they are often of decorative value, it is a matter of concern that a number have been lost in recent years, some by the effects of weather on the stone (which was often laid with bedding planes vertical and facing outward, making it more vulnerable). Some, though, have been lost or obscured by alterations to the buildings of which they are part. In three instances, this booklet offers a record of datestones that are now almost (or entirely) lost: see pages 22, 34 (sun-dial) and 44. A comprehensive record of all existing datestones, supported by photography, would provide valuable material for the history of the village.

A final "document in stone", reproduced opposite, is the gravestone of James Barker, mentioned earlier. It is to be seen under the trees on the southern edge of the churchyard, and stands alongside the gravestone of "Peter Barker, mason" (1749-1805) who, according to the parish register, died of "inflammation of the lungs", an occupational hazard of masons exposed to dust when cutting stone. He had three sons who were masons, James, Joseph and Peter II. The one commemorated here died at a relatively young age, probably when working in Skipton. Meanwhile, his brothers were listed among leading masons in the village in the 1822 directory quoted earlier, and are likely to have built several of the houses identified in these pages.

In MEMORY of
James Barker who departed
this Life January 1st 1814
Aged 44 years

16663626R00035

Printed in Poland
by Amazon Fulfillment
Poland Sp. z o.o., Wrocław